sifting

fire

writing

coast

Title: sifting fire writing coast / Elanna Herbert
ISBN 9780645797701
Cover image: Elanna Herbert

Publisher: Walleah Press
South Launceston
Tasmania, Australia 7249
www.walleahpress.com.au
ralph.wessman@walleahpress.com.au

In the spirit of reconciliation the author acknowledges the Traditional Custodians of country throughout Australia and their connections to land, sea and community. We pay our respect to their Elders past and present and extend that respect to all Aboriginal and Torres Strait Islander peoples today.

sifting
fire

writing
coast

Elanna Herbert

fire

sifting

coast

fire: *with your bright*

new

meaning

you bastard…

Fire Rites

Only these are my fire rites now
earned, stolen, still nurtured, long
worried, woven through past scars on
south country – this coast less frequently
burnt – the Spotted Gums forest, *Corymbia*
maculata, an *immaculata* of thick black
bark reeks raw another landscape
unexpected shadow of a European
fairytale winter emerges through
nightmare smoke, an Antipodean
summer: burnt.
forest, part healing, part lost
too soon. Extirpation events
nudged forward by a certainty
of collective indifference, rekindled
as collective sorrow, despite politicians'
self flagellation – deniers who: look
the other way. On the runway to Hawaii
chose Pacific clarity over our apocalypse
on an orange sky beach: blunt apology
for those of us who lay too close, too
soon, this sudden loss. Solastalgia
hits like a rock: bludgeoned.

Sit close by me silent forest, come share
my moonlight – peel off your
lizard skin of fresh burn, watch
as I rake coals – remember the falling
of soft black snow, burning leaves
caught on wind, a lightness of
desiccation so brittle it shimmered
the overheated air with a volatile
sickness. Light a candle. Breathe
the close comfort of wax melt. Watch
from my night deck, on the ridge line
your orange-red glow of still
burning trunks reignites us.
: incendiary.

Recalling a lightning strike near Exmouth

in low scrub. like the saltbush outside
my father's town, a release on the edge
of a continent

after that distance
from Perth.　　　looking back
to the interior
near Exmouth

hot wind a beach car park. beside the
splayed tyres of grey nomaded four wheel
drives and European campervans let out
to roam our toes are coral sand
grit. we Snapchat Cape Range. it

lies low settles into an afternoon
spent contemplating erosion. ahead
the storm lightning, smoke. a bushfire
in low scrub.

let it burn

the rutted man
in the car park said. raising his voice
near Exmouth

up here scrub has no value

up here the scrub is a canopy for snakes
near Exmouth

you step into silence, feel each place
as a spirit   each spirit
as a place   a *genius loci* which

Wikipedia tells me is a thing ancient Romans
worshipped and often depicted as a snake

but I'm just sayin' if
the rutted man
in the car park holding belief
firmly rusted a badge for all
the rutted men
near Exmouth

were to ask, I am sure there's
a woman perhaps there's an
Aboriginal woman, perhaps there's
many women, who would speak of
things sacred, beyond

                    has no value
to add to transient car park conversation
with the rutted men.
                    raising our voices
near Exmouth

Processing Afghan Asylum Seekers

it's like they've got each other's back
not just now but from way back
since the time of Genghis

you can spot the ones
who've spent
years in detention
they still walk slowly

energy saving
blue tee shirt
free flip flops
tracksuit pants
saying little
just the look

trying to forget the boat

they recognise the faces
of those who were there

the younger guys
arrive at the office in Perth
with more confidence
they like checked shirts
like the Indigenous guys
they never met up north
out from Derby

maybe the Hazara men
in detention got the fashion
message from those local
Aboriginal men through
the silver fence at Curtin
Detention Centre
carried on the red dust

that blew through some days
as the scrub burnt in the dry
and took the edge off the heat

or maybe wearing a checked shirt
is that bit of the West
the Taliban dislike so much

so the guys wear it
to convince themselves
that reporting to Immigration
every change of address
to keep a temporary visa
is what freedom looks like

Too Many Years a Railway Daughter

I wanted to step into the steam loco
touch it feel its heat steam soot: run
back to you and tell you it was ready to leave.
But I had already come such a long way
and you are fading into your past: your pride

makes it three generations
railway boys grew to railway men: four sons
shiftwork themselves into some kind of living
across three states crosscut by rails. The Sunday
4:15 travels just enough to feed a family.

This train eases past my childhood into the siding
all too familiar like stepping across the coupling's doorway
that gush of cold wind hard edged up through the gaps
so familiar I know the words, sounds, taste: of train

even the windows still open all the way down
and my teenagers already becoming bored look
jaded, confident their easy fantasy future assured

their glance says it all. We pass three
old houses close-by blue weatherboards
strung out along the line beyond the station
one already burnt to the ground: despair
so recent bits of no-go police tape tinsel the carcass
and a 1950s metal bathtub stands sentinel inside
a wall-less bathroom as I wonder about arson

I didn't bother to tell the kids these are
railway houses. That if we were to run
to the bottom of the garden at your brother's house
in your railway town, us kids could watch railway men shunting
the train leaving for Adelaide or Alice or Perth: that went

beyond saltbush out into no-man's land the train
Uncle Rex drove when he was away while
Uncle Cliff was the Stationmaster when
Uncle Ivan wasn't filling in as his father had
like you did for a while in another town: or tell them

that to edge a railway house garden use empty
beer bottles upturned in red desert sand
like it was another world or world's
end. The line that connects all stations.
This train at the end of the line.
Sunday afternoon at Dwellingup.

List of what to take when the fire arrives:

(cross out any which no longer apply)

Handbag, Wallet, Passport, Birth Certificate
Dad's 1950s silver serviette holders from Kosciuszko shaped
like skis
Dad's 1947 football trophy "Best Utility Player, S.F.C - B Grade"
Mum's silver sapphire engagement ring worn thin with age
Mum and Dad's wedding album
Dad's photos of ancestors I never met
That photo of Mum at 13 during the war with her hair back
Father-in law's war medals
My gold engagement ring (do you still need this? – let the
wedding ring burn)
The fire blanket
The P2 masks
The evacuation backpack
The dog's evacuation bag (don't forget her meds)
The dog
~~The King Parrot family raiding the veggie garden for green
tomatoes~~
That spot on the wooden lounge room floor which makes the
fibro wall creak when you step there on humid summer
mornings
The day I first stood on the redone deck (pack memory, forget
cost)
Dad's 8mm reels of 1960s home movies (should have been
copied by now)
The day me and Dad first viewed the house (of all my memories
of Dad why this one?)

The 1950s green glass light fitting in the end bedroom which
I found at the back of an old shelf in the garage
~~The smell of summer breakfast BBQs from the~~ ~~front deck~~
~~of the double story corner house.~~ ~~(Coco the~~
~~cat didn't make it out)~~
The widest view of the lake from the far corner of the deck
The smell of mozzie coils and white wine on the deck at night
~~The sounds of cattle bellowing from the~~ ~~paddock~~
~~across the road~~
~~The red cedar storybook cottage~~ ~~across~~
~~from us~~ ~~which my 8 year old daughter wanted to buy instead of~~
~~our house~~
Bluey the Bluetongue Lizard
The dining room off the kitchen where Mum and Dad and the
kids ate our first roast lamb dinner in the house (where's the
photo to prove this now?)
Skinky the tailless who lives under the back cement step
~~The Bower Bird family~~ ~~who raid~~
~~the dog kibble bowl at dawn~~
~~The Whip Bird~~ ~~calling~~
~~The late night possum who eats~~ ~~fallen~~
~~oranges in the back yard~~
~~The Kookaburra family who~~ ~~wake too~~
~~early in summer~~
~~The neighbours orange tree hanging overladen with fruit across~~
~~my back fence~~
~~The sound of the back neighbours van arriving~~ ~~home in~~
~~their driveway~~
The sunburnt children lying on mattresses on the floor of the
blue bedroom (pack this memory too)

The blue mosaic floor tiles which remind me of the ocean
~~The smell of rain when you stand on~~ the back porch
~~The small green valley~~ in Valley ~~Drive~~
The paintings from Bali and Kakadu (is tourist art important?)
The gouges in the lounge/ hallway/ back bedroom in the
Cypress Pine floor made by the kids /me /tenants /dragging
furniture /stiletto heels
The gaps in the lounge room floorboards where light comes
through when you open the garage door underneath the house
~~The view from my kitchen sink window to~~ the blue
~~loft house~~
~~Sound of fruit bats fighting in the nectarine tree of~~ the blue
~~loft house~~
The red cedar beams lined up in neat rows stepping along the
hallway ceiling
The huge red cedar support beam in the lounge room still
wrapped in tinsel
My brand new ceiling fans (pack the remote)
~~The communal mandarin tree in the front yard of the~~
abandoned house near the boat ramp
~~The neighbours orange tree in~~ the front yard of ~~their~~
~~holiday house~~
The sound of distant surf from the front deck at night
~~The sounds of children playing in~~ the driveway ~~of the~~
~~grey house~~
The moon shining ~~on the COLORBOND® roof of~~ the house
~~on the corner~~

~~The flowering Jacaranda in the garden of~~ ~~the house on the corner~~

~~The Yellow Tail Black Cockatoos calling as they fly overhead to the pine trees of~~ the green roof house by the lake

The red bricks on my ~~front garden~~ steps with "Canberra C'wealth" stamped on their face which Dad salvaged from a demo job.

~~The Superb Fairy Wren family who chirp and flit~~ ~~across my front garden each morning~~

My newly painted hallway, two coats of "Sea Mist", three days of hard work

~~The mopoke owl calling late at night from the~~ ~~ridge behind~~ the creek

~~The comings and goings~~

~~of the neighbours~~

~~as they go~~ about

their ~~lives~~

Whatever else you can fit in the car in 5 minutes.

Breathe.   Remember to use the mask.

on that morning

i was being/ ready/ ready being one parent/ i was being
sensible sister/ being a follower of the 5 safe steps/ i was being
follow the plan/ i was being clear/ clear away/ clear it/ clear
the decks/ prepare prep re are pre/ i was being pre/ fire/ i
was being hose it/ i was being sprinkler/ i was being water/
water/ i was being take/ albums/ i was being real/ reality
bites/ i was being it/ it was being chopper/ it was being
chopper buckets/ chopped up/ overhead/ it was being no
help/ no no help at all/ it was being orange clouds/ bill
billowing/ i was being can't believe/ is the this/ the big thing/
this it/ is fire/ The Currowan[1]/ i was being here/ being
fireplan/ i was being unreal/ i was being Hollywood/ movie/
i was being a disaster movie/ Apocalypse Now move move
movie/ i was being my own home movie/ my horror/ my red
hot horror movie/ it was being side red on our/ roadside red/
no/ it was being orange/ orange/ orange flames like water/
orange flames like water flowing down to/ it was being orange
water flames flowing downslope/ the green paddock/ it was
being catch the green paddock/ i was being mesmerised/

flames flowing in the paddock behind houses/ orange flames behind blue house across/ behind our street/ our street/ our street/ being at houses in our street/ i was being no/ not yet our/ burning Lakeside Dr/ burning tracks through the bush behind paddock/ burning near us/ the corner/ the here/ The Currowan burning/ it was/ being burning near the corner here/ i was being stay it/ stay/ calm it/ i was being don't panic/ don't panic/ i was being think/ think/ think it out/ i was being a gap/ next i think/ i was being a run/ i was being go/ go/ go now/ on that day i was being alive/ being South Coast/ i was being all South Coast/ it was here/

Far South

driving the tourist road to Narooma, life gets feral
outside Moruya. things relax, not me, just the locals.
the lady with the multicoloured hair, four loud colours
on the over 65's feels like one decibel too many. then
the girl in the organic veg shop waves me through, stays
on her phone, smiles as I tap and go. I expect nothing less
from a town where highway house gardens hold lambs close.

crossing Coila Creek, landscape folds like dry calico
no matter the time of year. at Tuross, I fail to arrive, boxes
kept firmly shut are flung open as Pandora's glorious
sea breeze, rolling up the hill, hits me with my mid '70s
summer – two teenagers on the beach. before you were killed.
before your seventeen should have arrived (despair never
lets me turn off to the lake). at Bodalla, much younger with

Mum and Grandma, my childish horror at finding a one
legged seagull on the cheese factory roof, Mum's joke about
where its leg went. summer of '69 bringing seagull not raven
as the harbinger of Grandma's own amputation, *mise en scène*
on the far south coast always collides with emotion, things stay
raw. too many ghosts lie in wait, or maybe childhood instinct, still
keen as a feral cat, reclaims, over and over our early coast trips

brazen simplicity. it's no wonder then, my lack of surprise
when I saw through a haze of smoke so thick that even
the television couldn't disguise its taste, the goat woman from
Cobargo wearing her black and blackened Led Zepp T-shirt
shouting at ScoMo, concisely shrinking him down hard, after
his ill-timed holiday to Hawaii and her fire fight that day
against a nightmare. impossible to comprehend.

Part of its trunk

and the root ball sit askew, looming out
of the socket created as it came down. these
roots reached the watertable, cracked
geology, broke apart sandstone of this
once river valley, to suck old moisture
laid down before the word geology was
even

a thing. the root ball will lay here for the last
few hundred years of the tree's existence, until
thick charcoal flakes off, and rot sets in, to pull
away from warm soil, lurching sideways
the decapitated head of a triceratops in
a Hollywood disaster movie. a scene not that out
of place

right now. in the forest behind, stands one thin
trunk, caught alone this sapling must have gone off
like a roman candle, the branchless dead
tree twists into a pull of liquorice, a stick
of charcoal, ready to sketch the scene. how brittle
I imagine, if it were smaller and fitted neatly in the
palm

of my cupped hand. I walk on, still hunting the old
track through fallen branches and leaf drift thick
like sea foam, negotiating clear footfall with this
endless burnt forest. here and there tufts of new growth
push up green and red to the surface, flailing sideways from
trees with energy left for regrowth. it feels too soon for
this assertion

of life. too soon to bury the dead. but it is done, and here
I stand still trying to grasp at flames to unravel this cliché
of disaster. apocalypse was a word which smoothed the
introduction of strangers at the evac centre next day, was
whispered while roaming the streets like startled 'roos looking
out for their mob, once we were allowed back in. here on
what was

the track, I stand where memory, my unreliable narrator
tells me I first saw fire arrive, when I saw flames flow like
water, burning orange-fast downhill. visceral is the word
I covet now, the unimagined made real. mesmerising orange
fire, its stark beauty tantalising me that thought, the split
second beckoning a decision: stay: watch this unfold as if
it was

a sunset moment caught between clouds, when light
breaking through unexpectedly hits one side of a tree
washing it sharp, rare beauty making you give thanks for the
moment. only not that day – when a body reacts
instinct tracing nerve endings returns our biological
inheritance – as if flight or
fight

is a clear eyed rationality, an idea a mind could form
when an avalanche of flames screamed the opposite
of the propaganda caught in our throats: that a bushfire
will travel fastest going uphill, and a downhill slope
will slow flames down. only not that day, not
that day.

after the fires, i cannot

get enough of the smoke
from your smoking ceremony into my hair
eyes, lungs coming up my legs snake tendril
hands grasp smoke desire to
cleanse. me, us, them, we, this
coast. it would be the Indigenous way
is what Conjola Bendalong Yatte Yattah
Jerrawangala Wandandian Malua
Broulee Mogo Nelligen: so many
this summer, my past south
and present coast, beg us. here, down
on one knee, gasping for us to hear
this fire ready country, fire adapted
fire endemic, pyrophytes grown
to it — moth to a flame
is a cliché — eucalypt to a flame
is this country my ancestors landed on
dangling their fancy convict chains, millstones
around their necks, their ploughs and thick
German bread. dragging European hearths to
a land of fire long owned (on landing
we somehow overlooked that concept). now
we avoid ignore, perilously override, choose
to forget. adjust our paradigm
'she'll be right', not so innocently
snigger at racist rednecks while ignoring

deeper knowledge, that word snigger
s... n word – just what is the root there?
we flood the halls with climate deniers on voting day
only to sweep them out and convert the evac
centre to disaster recovery, fashion
hippy earth mothers into retro beach
style – just what is *Boho* anyway? all that
macramé does my fuckin' head in. nothing
is ever that easily pale pastel washed, soft
toned keeping it neat, keeping it nice, no
discomfort, no defacing the
paradigm as we shift the cliff edge
just that little bit further away
until too late. i cannot
get enough of this smoke out

Pyrocumulonimbus

my disaster movie relives
a scene illegitimate on New Year's Eve
our *mise en scène* for a year of flame

everywhere lapping
a south coast summer — orange tides
rise high over memory

> ferocity cuts
> the air. a knife slices the day
> in two
> before: after
> fire

speed height wind heat noise smell taste choking
the bile in the gut. the grit in the eye. chaos. this
living stalking thing. *The Currowan.*

you
make your own
weather.

clouds burn smoke overhead
ignite air over land
throw fireballs
at fence posts. your wind
strips ash horizontal flows

across paddocks. in gullies you build
power. forests bring lightning
for its own sake
collapse flames
to implode a house   strip the powerless

tell me

           unreliable narrator. tell me
           I first saw fire

arrive
in my street.   these lapses
are gaps of trauma
distilled.   no one had this movie down

the way it was meant   to be played
still slow flames here
         under my skin.

When the first rain comes

It is pathetic.
Thin, patchy, the phlegm
of an old man worn
out with coughing.
Unproductive.

Where was this two weeks ago?

Now, the burnt land
sops it up, trickles it to the creek
with distain. Even the lake is
flaccid, flagging, foul. Fire weary.

Rain - this pathetic latecomer, with the temerity to
crawl, into COLORBOND® carcases of homes, softening
asbestos sheeting splintered into myriad pieces of
'70s coastal modernism, to layer rust over

the remains of cars, which pissed out
their aluminium in a gust
of heat
when left alone, parked on
the street, in the garage, alongside the pile
of bricks which was the side of a house.

"Too late to leave" - has no meaning as I piece
together our steps on that day with the remains of fire's
tracks. I should read its path, but I have no
Indigenous connection with country. I never learnt fire.

Much to my disgrace. And this rain will wash over
tracks, too soon a blush of green will obscure
the fear
until the wind picks up iron roof slabs, balanced
delicately, a child's school project, folded steel cardboard

over a brick laundry of the house next door. The once
roof creaks and groans each opportunity it gets, taken
by a glance of breeze. These are:

ship's noises in a disaster movie, just before she sinks
drowning the crew in a flood of water as it
crashes through the scorched wound
which was the hull.

Firepit

Today two Bower Birds discovered my stolen
iron firepit, holding this dichotomy firmly
by the rim, simultaneously fire and water. The
male glorious as ever in satin, midnight blue.
Iridescent. The female camouflaged, a piece of

soft green speckle, jittery, drinking at her new
waterhole. The large rusted pit barely balances
leaning drunkenly to the left, defiant in its metal
support ring, as stout as a dockers' shop steward
now two of its three legs bend backwards. I took the pit

soon after the ashes had cooled. Only a small re-birth
part of one house in my street, architect designed and
listed on 'Stayz'. A neighbour saw its walls pulse in
smothering. Then out. Sudden. Explosive. Facebook
showed me the ball of ragged orange colour, a gap

where a house should be as bushfire porn. Just
thankful now, I don't have the acrid smell of that
memory scarring my delicate cornea. I once said
no house deserved the misfortune to be built
on that block — a swampy site which flooded

regularly when the creek rose – but once finished
it looked great, despite the slope. Raised on stilts
channelling a tropical getaway, more Byron Bay than
Conjola, all white and terraced, plenty of intimate
decks, views north to bush, east the lake, magnolia

and jacaranda trees growing well, a white gardenia
hedge matched the walls. How ironic it all ended
the way it did. I dug the pit out, a recognisable
object – figured someone should keep it – then
I dragged it home, before contractors arrived

to crush the remains, as cremated bones
are crushed after a funeral, to fit neatly into
pewter urns. People don't know that fact:
what's left of their loved ones' bones are crushed
by a machine, after the fuss of ceremony and

the smooth departure behind the velvet curtain.
Family tears just a precursor to a process of
machine-led destruction, another reason I voted
for burial. The firepit once sat on an expensive
sandstone hearth, at the back, under well-designed

decking, there was a kettle nearby, still shining
resting on coils of rusting mattress wire, with
pieces of crushed bathroom glass fused by heat
slumped beside a melted shower-screen frame, nearer
the street, bolts from the car deck lay along the ground

still studded neatly into rows. I never understood how
much metal goes into building a beach house. With
the pit safely in my backyard, I spoke to the owner, on
her last visit before the yellow "For Sale" arrived
to the block. "Keep it" she said "Better you than the

demo truck". Then she too, left. Salvage is the word
birds here now drink from. Their family once much
larger. I remember the females, pre-fire, each
dawn squabbling with beaks deep in the dog kibble
bowl, always so many of them. Eventually they took

turns, then left. The male arrived alone, swooping
in only after his ladies had finished. Precariously
near to overflow, the inside bell curve of the pit
with its past of holding fire (both intended and
unintended) now cradles this weight of iron

rich water, slowly steeping a dichotomy
of disaster, grown more useful in its second life
a resurrections of sorts, part of the resurrection of
things. Burnt pits from a life, to give life. Survivors.
Today two Bower Birds.

For three days now, or is it

fourteen: men have worked smashing five last pieces
of house across the road using machines whose names
I will never know ridden by jockeys with names
twisted into jokes, inverted descriptions or just plain
bastardry: Goofa, Wazza and the little Blackduk,
names called from the driver's seat or at the local
when its time to shout your mate, to knock off, to
bond in blokedom after a hard day onboard the
cement cracking thing, the orange digger claw thing,
the tipper, the bob cat and the trucks, after a hard day
repeating these crushing actions over and over, like a
fighter in a bare knuckle fight, Sullivans Creek after
school one hot summer's

day: when Lyneham High boys took on the Catholics
from 'Dara' once and for all a bunch of them beating
and kicking down the thing they despised, the thing
they feared was better than them but could never say
so outside the rugby pitch, actions the same as the
machine jockeys these fourteen days beating and
smashing and kicking down hard into the remains of
homes, over and over into downed loved ones hit hard
in that firestorm of a NYE party which never ended
when 000 the police ambulance and RFS were called
but no one arrived: and now another is down on its
knees, it remains beside two others which fell to the
ground together like puppies, belongings scattered over

each other, the wooden cedar one, the blue storybook cottage one, a grey which used to be pink, the expensive architect white one which pulsed then exploded, and fuck do they really need that many trucks reversing at 06:15, I hope those machine jockeys in orange and yellow fluoro on the traditional navy blue base, blue as dark a shearer's singlet that old-school uniform of class and grit, I hope they just drive far

off: into a western sunset in their utes, shouting their long goodbyes, the classic way a man might do, or more likely melt into the pubs and pitfalls of town to sink a beer at the back end of the week, I could go to town now put on some tight black jeans and watch them walk into the pub with its nice new deck, like lost souls returning from 2019's Deni ute muster walking away from a day of destruction with a slap on the back and a joke about how easy their victims fell never really putting up a

fight: instead I know tomorrow or the day after or the day after that, watching from my deck across the road I will see Mal in his black dual cab ute drive past the gap in our street where his house once stood, the one he finished building himself just before his new partner gave birth to his last child, his second time round family, back when he still had one chance left to build a dream and when it was finished to sink a beer sitting on his deck on a hot day wearing his dark blue singlet back before chaos razed a fire trail to our village

Re/ main/ s

living post apocalypse is anger
bouncing from one disaster to the next
survival mode, adrenalin caressing
neurons, partying the amygdala to action
the rush leaves gaps of memory and those

images of horror you drive past each day
welcoming the abhorrent as your familiar
you gently stroke it, until a sudden corner
angle, position, grows fresh, new tears held
in reserve drawn from the well, you grip

the steering wheel, breathless.
now I get it. those brick ghosts
monuments of isolation. now
I understand where lonely farm
chimneys come from, out west

or east – as you drive a barren
landscape, and think WTF is that doing
there? here, South Coast chimney stories
begin amid burnt metal, fused pots
scattered china, melted glass. here lie the

re/ main/ s of cast iron wood heaters held in situ
hearths still the heart of the home, standing
drenched by rubble, growing from remains
like the yellow sunflowers planted each spring
by the dairy farmer's kids, on the road verge

as you drive south up Stony Hill, in Milton
where the first roadblock was set
before lunchtime on fire day

This naked lake rests

i

after the fires: she is shamed, her corset of trees flayed
denuded. this naked lake no longer settles: she is
restless despite the new rise
orange blood moon

ii

spring swallows return, seek familiar eaves, nest in lost houses
the gaps now staining their valley. do swallows imagine
a concept of apocalypse as they breathe continuum
fly confused by absence?

iii

the cutaway for the new retaining wall holds no lies, a layer
of ash, carbon of recent burn, otherwise glutinous clay
layered by rich alluvial terrace – and us here living the
first hard burn – ten thousand years to mark this soil
has climate change brought you clarity yet?

iv

before loss: 1962 drew a coastal village. lake views sliced blocks
from a stolen dairy paddock woven through a sideways riff of
Spotted Gum bush: now silent, regrowth thick, epicormic. this
once was, in the time of shellfish and fish traps. of ochre and song.
the time of story, if you have a mind to listen to the Yuin

v

in the flood no one believes a fury of fire, imagines the day
a nightmare, buries it quick in softer rain, before South Coast
returns its autumn: in mist this naked lake wraps herself close,
disappears beyond Killarney, with the distance of hill becomes
Scottish Loch, shifts her gaze, glances east where

vi

Cunjurong Point belies Caledonian provenance, washing the surf
break – a left-hander, staying long off Green Island – across the
broken sandbar inside Conjola Island, lost in sand beside Princess
Island, Oyster Point remembers shellfish popping on hot coals
the chatter of children up past Picnic Bay, to Conjola Creek.

vii

this lake twice drowned by river valleys, folded by creek
still marked in change. calm bays lay down
before fire, naked, stripped
by flame.
this lake

Sifting: *examine*

                       all parts

                  separate useful, from

                         discard

descend sparsely as if sprinkled from a sieve.

                     something else

        claw fingers through ... dust ...retain
                          coarse

The Yass Fossils

i am holding time
sifting silted silence
weighed down by memory
synapsed. my thought
processes stumble
through Yass, in the EK Holden

and the fossils. that summer (1969)
i wrote magic names only we could
understand: trilobites, brachiopods
Derringullen creek, Grabben Gullen
under a railway bridge and
Shearsby's Wallpaper at the top

of someone's paddock. i remember worrying
about the cliff, the scattered points of quartz
stones and finding amethyst. its clarity near
the desiccated corpse of a fallen cow (i kicked
at bones)
things you don't find in books. being with Dad

in the year i discover Science, things new
exciting, close. i became important, almost
a real thing, when he took me and the boy
next door to visit Science. we saw a moon rock

crowded by people looking to drink the future
but all i found was a forlorn thing at the centre of
a crowd – no gracious lunar bead – irregular quite
dull, insignificant. there Dad bought me a book

with a booted footprint stepping down onto grey
dust. a thing of the moon. of Science. after Dad
is gone there is no one to ask why we did that
summer of fossil hunting. just this thought now

dug up – laid bare – this must have been
it. that moment he decided i was enough to
substitute for his unborn son – so he showed
me things he couldn't understand
and i believed him. now i Google rocks

kept locked in a pink painted
box – *stigmaria ficoides*, a club moss root
– *spinella brachiopod* – *odontopleura*
trilobite. hear. these. names. Science names
(never our names) things of stone things

of plant of shell the chitin fallen to
mud carbon to stone. they never were
                                    the skins of dinosaurs.

Digging the block

I remember the crunch fall
of clay baked hard packed
lifeless all through the dry years

or heavy and waterlogged
revealing rich colours
grey ochre and deeper down vivid

              richest yellow
orange streaked smooth between my
fingers slippery cold-frost. The acidic sharp
smell of Yellow Box leaf fall mixed with

another like the taste of clear water
              before

it pools   travels across softening earth
picking up a tinting of bare patch run-off silt.

And wet cold rain.   Blizzard rain so you knew
without a doubt
          up in the Brindi's[3]
          the first drifts of snow.

The Trap

I remember the trap
and the sharp smell of rust
long finished it hung
on the wall

creosote and memory
strange that here
they remain soft
bundles of recollection

the trap and a crosscut saw

where they hang still
rust slabs of curing meat
along the fly blown walls
of his old garage

near the tartan car seat

where my sleeping sister
was lifted up
from the back seat

of our old EK

Near the Sphinx

in Egypt, a Bedouin beggar woman's child is
shugged on the hip of her mother. a worn satchel

jaded by life – spent before she can walk – is she the
subaltern as a child? My Postcolonial sensitivities don't

stretch to a dusty lunch outside this aircon haven of the
Colonel's KFC. The child's mother, washed by desert heat

gestures outside the restaurant window, puts her hand to
her mouth, stares at me with that weird beggar woman stare

I can't turn away from, like the stare of the Afghan girl on
the cover of an old *National Geographic*: Sharbat Gula

when they found her name, was living a refugee life as
a dead woman's child in Pakistan, before she was sent

home at thirteen for her war wedding. And my KFC tastes
stale, oily, sits in my mouth. I distil privilege.

Pompeii

Hora prima

...do you remember...

Long grasses move in a silent breeze

It was you who took me there.

and the lizards, green and brown

We walked in separately.

part quickly over the silent

That was the morning.

stones.

Long grasses move in a...

Road to Gallipoli: between Cappadocia and Pamukkale

I remember 1977   the day after Pamukkale or the
day before forty degrees in the shade me and Heather
climbed down a gully beside the road to a shallow river a
big creek with rocks

            I got totally wet in that river

lying down   in creek water shallow in my
brown cotton cross-over straps sun dress cheap leather
sandals I haggled well back in Greece I immersed my body
fully water flowed over my head my torso my between my
legs I wanted to take that heat off undress my top layer of
skin peel peel it back reveal fresh flesh all I wanted to do
was to just cool down

            I wanted to think about you

walking up   the side of the steep bank dust
dry rocks treacherous inclination careful not to slip
climbing up that gully coming back to you dripping wetness
over you sitting in the dust three Kiwi mining mates strung
out in Turkey with heat and hangovers smoking sitting
beside the road sitting waiting looking hot being hot
complaining about how hot Turkey turned out to be after
the disappointment of Greece

            you looked up at me

standing wet   beside the road you said I looked like
a wild Gypsy like one of the women we had seen the day

before near Pamukkale probably Bedouin walking camels
and kids your blue blue eyes watched my wet cotton dress
cling tight against my body I held your gaze the broken
down bus was fixed I climbed on board sat beside you next
to the window watched the gully beside the shallow river
fall away the distance beyond you retreat I sat
wet through.

I felt cool refreshed.   Then we drove to Gallipoli.

Cursive Lessons

                    I am
writing this on
the back of that letter.

I write naked in the space
of my past   the
parchment stretched between
bones of my dreaming
the blank white space of it.

        Her finger dipped into the dark
indigo-blue bottle
delicious bottle of ink like the first time
she held the nibbed pen and learnt
the lessons of cursive.

            In those early years
she wrote clear and precise

she wrote the ink letters on his naked back
the blank white space of it.

The pen tip of her index finger
dragged across the skin's horizon
curling the letters where required
pressing the nail down sharply
each letter ending with a dark point.

She tattooed the letters of her past into flesh
and sent the letters off.

She did not expect
a reply
or anticipate
the blank white space of it

In the vault

of things lie the remains of that summer. old photographs are a slap in
the face. blue, faded. *wasted days and wasted nights.* once I thought

to transcribe Greece: cicadas, heat, the Aegean, Paros bathed
in luminosity complete as a page from a Durrell novel, but that

was Corfu, this was life. my diary of thin pages, a self absorbed grit
of weather, food, mundane travel debris. things are never as they seem.

even then. once I thought to paint a watercolour of Naoussa harbour: blue
boats, whitewashed houses, magenta bougainvillea, the road to the

taverna. I carried that photo until I lost it somewhere, then remembered
it takes a lifetime to forget. once I thought to write words: glorious

with sensuality, re-draw those seventies tattoos on tanned arms or
frame a touch, to watch reality falling, falling. to start again at the

beginning. instead I remember ruins, all the history of the world laid out
before us, carved up, an easy to digest package tumbling upon us waiting

waiting to be acknowledged. but all we could do was get drunk on cheap
ouzo, spend nights in backpacker sex, aimless days talking life

to come, surrender to cool Mediterranean tides too early for the
real season, watch sunsets burn night at the wired disco. I met some

French guys, you spent the night with an older woman. next day at
the market I bought cheap leather sandals. I haggled. I learnt the way

of things. you sent a postcard home to a girlfriend. I watched you write
may as well be here as anywhere. we drank hedonism to slake our

thirst, forgot the beautiful promise of youth, ate *hubris* in a clear
morning distilled by ancient Greeks at the taverna, the ones waiting

for us to learn the price. once I thought the impossible: back in
touch and delirious with survival we got drunk, watched sunsets

burn an ocean from your balcony, ate seafood on a beach, talked
labyrinths of life yet to come, had sex, drove north, bought wax

for our wings. forgot the payment. no one is ever the first
to fall. even now, learning of your death

Aubie: Kokoda: 1988

after the ambulance
the final rush from home
swept up by your past
your breath your war
the coma begins. short.

sharp. rattles of phlegm
covet the vastness your
unchosen experience your
retelling untold

crinkle sheets hospital sterile
wrap the remains of memory
around a wasted body. coma

inductions strong as birthing
surface pull terror up clutching
clots of humid night thoughts your
war distils over a horizon
seeps into whiteness a
Canberra Hospital room cold
beyond the July freeze. we wait
slowly. occasionally fidgeting. drawn

into fear your life's end echoes
battle foetid Kokoda
Ioribaiwa Oivi Gona
strange murmurings

mates' cries your reply
their unheard calls our
witness. your chosen
breath shouts. sharp.
short. useless as pain at lungs
drowning lungs
dying is never that
moment. you prepare.

Today we should have

been at that *warung* in the Kuta laneway
eating *Gado-gado*. the one we went to
last time when you told the kids *Ratus*

ratus crawling along the rafters was
an Indonesian marsupial and my teenage
daughter ordered Shepherd's

Pie because for once she missed her
mother's cooking. instead we buried our
father in the grave of our mother. we threw

disjointed flowers from my garden onto
exposed soil. their bruised colour held down
her bones. then two daughters, a granddaughter

the tall cousin from Sydney and the grandson
carried our father's coffin to her place overlooking
the ocean. we stood together. we watched

his coffin lowered into her earth. and that moment
rolled in breaking with emotion as we threw the last
of my winter flowers on top. later at the club we both

ordered pepper steak, a white wine. he knew
this routine. we sat. we watched. the ocean.

Coast: *Great Southern Reef   King tide   Pacific*
Indian   Ocean
coastline extends
inland to the first major change in terrain

aqua clear
honeycomb cliffs

bodysurfing

the blue of

humidity &
coral
bay

sea kissed   glassy

Lake Conjola

read the reflection

in the January king tide
lake stars float on a surface
of black oil infinity water

big diamond little diamond
phosphorescence

                    phosphorescence dancing a spangle
                    of stars I recall moments the

Giotto ceiling Scrovegni chapel
I never did visit with you and the unnamed
artist another chapel

Deir el-Bahari, Hatshepsut the Queen's ceiling stars the
        weight of limestone pressing down held tight by lapis

crushed blue gems woven solid pressing up a layer
of three thousand years balanced
unwavering in intensity
there I breathed the sublime
inhaled the detritus of mummification

left   melting into the sun barely here
              I return pick up pieces of life at
Lake Conjola white stars reflect liquid
night slides them under the jetty
to return out the other side held

by tidal flow crushed charcoal tints of moonlight a carpet
of light points bright on dark, like a pub floor design swirling
reflecting those points so strong after a couple of drinks you
believe you could stand on it
          that it would silently hold your weight.   walk through

          my cosmos the
          lake edge the
          surface at night
          each diamond a universe of positionality
          splintering white-light thoughts

fear keeps its distance
tonight it is just me and the lake stars
dancing on the jetty's edge

Greenpatch Beach

mothers sisters daughters
spring warmth bickering
with the summer sun

our day went softly walking
on feather clouds raised
images an artist's book

the pages from that day
overlaid with tempera
resonating stillness

structure you might say.
Lines taken for a walk
through generations. Women

close knit with texture.
You held her arm steady
grandchildren behind

at last we arrived back
at the car left behind
sea's distilled waves

a soft wash of Seahorse tails
butterfly kissed the shore
stretched canvas tight

before them. Greenpatch
your Dreamtime Spirits
shone: shine: flaunt

Port Jackson sharks
who sweep rock ledges
with innocence below

baubles of spring weed
miniature bubble bladders
adrift on an ancient tide.

Then I wonder like those
Seadragons we came upon
when snorkelling you turn

and point for a sister's
eyes to share but pushing
against the current next

years spring tide, you look
back, they are gone.

Washerwomans Beach

her dappled road swings hard, drawn equally to both sun
and shade, the road verge an energy company's ripping
project, insurance for next time, pass the sign for

'Slow Wombats' hand-painted by someone with wombat
passion drawn by wombat loss, those bright young
wombats who die alone, discarded like overturned

footstools on the road verge, making us look away from
road kill carnage to contemplate ecosystem collapse. this dappled
road leads to a dappled track. park in the shade of a *Stayz* tree

on the way to the headland (a peak feverishly sought by jaded
tourists) across the clearing's long grass watch for snakes as
you shimmy past the Council 'track closed' sign. two years of

inaction on bushfire damage. now the track starts to dip, eroded
by storm runoff and weed regrowth, dappled with post fire
thistles, seeds from Scottish refugees find moist soil in this

La Niña summer, step over braided tree roots, the black
trunked survivors still embedded in their ecozone. those who
endure, remain. here at the track convergence dappled by

dips and shadows, hollows and ghost rocks, my indecision on
the cross track never taken as new saplings flaunt chaos amidst
re-growth, the distant buzz of a jet ski throbs and the understory

of green bracken fern, fresh with curl, posits meaning to violet
Hardenbergia tendrils, as pea flowers weave a pastel tartan
over flax grass seed heads nodding low (so useful once to

Yuin women) now pea flowers move to dance like daffodils
in a Wordsworth poem, the famous one from that far away
land (grown irrelevant with colonisation). but right here at

Washerwomans her track makes windows laced through
tree trunks to intersect a triple layer horizon: sky sea land.
our beginning, middle and end, multiple sheets of turquoise

intersect as if some part of Queensland has fallen south for
just a moment and tripped itself up on Washerwomans' track
showing us her postcard colours, glorious and clear. a sudden

sweet salt smell of sea-close floats up the embankment, following
the track uphill it announces your arrival. while between her trees in
this glory of Queensland blue, her white caps shimmer, slice and

fall as shards of blue kaleidoscope into glass-green waves.
filaments of seaweed float, immerse as beached seaweed steeps
summer into dimethyl sulphide, rotting algae lifted up, and here

on the beach the evidence remains, lying between tourists
and their dogs. those tell-tale signs of inaction, of change. those
familiar burnt logs, the charcoal sticks, the salt drenched dark

flotsam of a south coast burn, debris only now ageing to grow
toward echoes of eventually. rolled by a thousand waves, a thousand
sighs, they persist. everything finds its way, eventually. to the sea

Anniversary, 2023

And the salt breeze, coming
up the estuary sweeps light
the deck bringing summer
to its peak, distils night

cricket calls echo the loaded
scent of wood smoke, tonight
instead, a lake tide settles, pops
seaweed to run under a battered

jetty, the way you stare down
the burn. Somewhere nearer, on
the edge of regrowth chaos, a
red-bellied black snake stirs, brings

movement in leaf litter, rock crevices
damp earth, then settles. Above her
a relief of storm clouds layer horizon
stars, scumble charcoal down

from sky's ceiling. Know that
tomorrow we will see: rain
the communion of early morning
beach swims, later tennis.

Mettams Pool

if you could run your fingers across this place
of sea and sand salt-bush laying on a scent of pepper
you will find my edge delineated in sea-glass

aqua clear marine bejewelled emerald inset with
ultraviolet flashes as shadow falls to liquid sapphire
if you could run your fingers across this place

swim stroke breathe wave breathe surf breathe dive
taste salt summer silt cocooned within this space
you will find my edge delineated in sea-glass

sunlight filters fool's gold flecks shimmers of
silver patterns lines flow solitude I float drift
if you could run your fingers across this place

sink blood sink body sink diamond light refracted
clear to my centre a salt-moist ocean it is there
you will find my edge delineated in sea-glass

to ache with the necessity of breathing of breath
interrupting water's grace of certitude. here. breathing
you will find my edge delineated in sea-glass
if you could run your fingers across this place

Sydney to Perth: chasing dusk

even in the air we breathe this land
of dust. a sliced horizon gashed orange
you might imagine the distant glow of fire.
just not this time. a sunset flattens land
already worn flat. I could weep

for a mountain now. but those days
are long gone. just this, a worn
pink continent. eternally making dust.
wallowing in its own drought. the self
pity of climate change, too dry

to shed a tear. I almost hear
the earth's curve. almost cross into
a concept through Western Australia
the southern land. from South Australia.
the driest state, the driest. some histories

never change. above, away from the barren
coast, flying into colours of an Italian ceiling
dust layers float on each another like horizontal
tree rings. colour grows luminous, tears itself
away from earth, to become atmospheric

rings of Giotto blue dust. sky saturates us
drowning tones of cardinal red, the fire
orange – blue. out beyond wind farms near
an idea called Whyalla (a place I once visited with
my father when long road trips were a thing) his gulf

coast's littoral keeps fading into dusk. the horizon
glow always stays that little bit ahead. it likes
that we never reach it, teasing us this surreal moment
spaces between days. cities. lives. inserting dusk
between the movie and the cardboard stew.

blue extends itself now, flexing its muscle: azure
cerulean, clear sapphire, cobalt, royal, ultramarine, navy
midnight, Prussian, indigo. need I say more? it sits heavy blue –
pressing down it grows darker, becomes the cliché of
nightfall. orange has already compacted itself into a thin

horizon somewhere below us. autocorrect is killing my words
wants me to speak corporate, worldly. no space here for
non-linear thinking. for flights of fancy tipping the paradigm.
just this thought rising to follow darkness – behind us night paves
down into drying coastal plains: even in the air, we swallow dust.

South Australia is mauve flowers

on quartz red sand Spinifex ringworms of new
growth outside my Father's town blown tyres dead 'roo lies
prostrate gestures at nowhere in his harsh light green
saltbush grey parallels a road edge along a childhood flash
the EK Holden the smell of heat the first long shimmer of
mirage/   above

Brown Falcons circle patiently awaiting the feast
their timeless gaze fixed there again the town arrives
sudden from nothing corrugated iron roof brown bottle
garden of sand and blue blue house blue sky blue water
blue gulf hills lizard thick shingle smooth blue your clawed
feet splayed underbelly lies low and warming close to the
female earth dark faces compact memory cool water tank
shades a past of silence of us and them those parks we must
not play not ever again Aunty said/   red sand

creeps slowly over skin folds of a flesh crevasse
veranda lattice screens canvas cool painted porch doors
shut out ovens of desert white heat first taste of orange
blossom smells salt and dust and flies and language and you
old lady/

east...west....east.....west......east.......west.........east

just listen listen to the space here again Perth
again tell it to me straight yet again yet again the
house the mess the mortgage the divorce & do not
speak text words & do not read: spaces between
lines pauses in the room classical music Gibbney
style & space & light & air neighbours polished
floors Jarrah & rugs chiaroscuro the piano &
space & light & air how like them to be from WA
to be from here never to be here to never be of
here of it of the soil just to be in WA be West be
Heat Light Space someone would say it when you
see the sign at the airport & home is Perth

so far home flying across a continent

into Conjola: Sydney airport freeway highway
fruit bats & lakes night surf wedged between
mosquitoes in the caravan & the front bunk room
Burrill summer humidity tell it to me straight yet
again yet again the tropical garden life & the man
tropical garden man i doubt he exists now just a
space i imagined once caught between the
corrugated iron of the old walls the house the
warm earth path between banana trees & palms
Black Cockatoos butterflies & bats there of course
would be bats & a life a night steamy tropic-dark
night & thin stars thin stars not like here reality

drives the Pilbara kids Auski Roadhouse is this
the outback cliché stars are diamond bright & wild
cattle run on cool grass near the bore
so   *far*   *home*   *flying*   *across*
a continent

in Gundaroo: a paddock once home past home no
home i watch the kids at night take them outside
step into space so familiar the milky way lays a
crisscross against the night sky diagonally
dragging horizon trees up from the dark lined
edge of the block across the clay dirt road where
neighbours still move their mob of sheep lambs to
the horse paddock near the creek plant dianella
stop erosion this is where the night sky flares
bright not the tropics not by a long shots
so   *far*   *home*   *flying*
across a continent

into Perth: coming back being back plant the
suburb night garden where the sand shocks me so
easy to dig so thirsty so thirsty wanting more
always wanting more the man next door who
doesn't own a boat tells me he says thirsty soil
over here we've got thirsty soil so don't dig the
subconscious to any great depth just leave it put it
up on the shelf & leave it put it on the mantelpiece
there pallid waiting just for now Inglewood I was
in love with your mantelpiece intimacy like home

grandmothers house one of mine take your pick
Sydney or

so   far   home

flying across a continent

in Port Augusta: like I walked into my childhood
and it fell apart around me & my daughter slides
the hallway in a school uniform she rejects & the
peppercorn tree hard slaps her 1950s fibro
bedroom wall late into the night neighbours ignore
a single mum so new she can't even pronounce
Mandurah move again get a house plant a garden
tell it to me straight yet again yet again my thirsty
garden thirst so thirsty it wants more always
wanting more wedged between a neighbour who
owns a boat & hates trees & a neighbour without a
boat who speaks truth thirsty soil always
wanting   more

so far home flying
across a continent

Albany Whaling Station

walking through
the abandoned whaling station
ordered equipment
vats and machines silent

shadowed by absence of song
bones bleached preserved
we admire their other-world
symmetry

the stench of progress
suffocates the sea's breath
like wet muslin wrapped
tight across my face

we struggle with meaning
a paradox of outdated technology
sepia wash coalescing into
faded images of the hunt

the feast of flesh and
feats of men skilled at
wielding the flensing knife
hanging unspoken

between us this
carcass of questioning
awaits an answer
so vast leaving a

gap in the oceans
we almost did
fall through

Whitford Nodes Park: what I hear

                    I should know these
west coast birds by now   should
have their dance and call
and patterns of being embedded
in my reckoning of place, but

carried on the wind only parrots
throw a true sound the Rainbows' screech
flaunts a familiarity parallels my
south coast days honey
and water and bread Mother's sunshine
and nectar days carried

on the wind rises stronger
falls restlessly seeks dominance
dominion tugs pushes hard between you
and me physical like days in a Tassie gorge
that wind didn't bother with simple

metaphors like screamed or howled
that wind came up through the gorge
late at night drunk and dangerous a harlot's
lover spurned feeling edgy busting for a fight
but here a beach winter's daylight filtered

and carried on the wind plays with edges
which contain delineate between
inland desiccation and coastal flux
trapped in a west coast grove pinned down
by lorikeet flocks and the relentless clatter
families breeding.

Perth Heatwave

Tonight the heat is down from the Pilbara
Karijini or Shark Bay.
Settling here.   You can smell it fall

heavy with dry air and dust like
a Tim Winton novel clever
people read, thinking they
imagine the West. It's nearly

midnight   nearly Easter.
I still need two showers a day.

Tonight the heat is down from the Pilbara
my suburb night-sweats silence. Today
felt like a photo, faded apricot

in your 1970s album that one I

        once saw

    you   a teenager lanky
the bro   your Dad's grave
that photograph on the page before me.

Stark cliffs bleed the camera lens red
a blonde stands in blue water. She
faced the camera. Was she the one
whose husband found out?

Tonight the heat is down from the Pilbara
heat you lived when Hedland was new
no rules   no consequences.
I remember you wore that with pride.

Now, your grown children polish the past.
Bigger houses reflect brittle lives
still waiting for the heat to
subside. For things to turn. She stands

recites her mantra, deftly
chimes hope   but already
the downturn   the layoffs
the   lies.   Excoriation.

Tonight the heat is down from the Pilbara
the red-eye tracks over Dianella, a police
siren cuts that hard line down Morley Drive

my ceiling fan shifts rhythm, airless
against the lack of flow

Stairway to the Moon: Roebuck Bay

tonight

it is the same moon I see now
sky moon sea merge end beat the day
with a night void of the sea's
breath of sand and weed stone
rock and curve

of the moon beach   of your tide

it is the same moon up in the north
the night dark wine
moon-peach full with
                    promise poignant with red

memories of dust tinged dry

                    this is that thing

the stairway moon that I
buried each day   you
                    were not here

Flying W.A.

the Indian Ocean brings the
abrupt line   aquamarine fades
cut with pale calico dark riparian
tendrils snake mangrove green
across my palette red
copper burnt sienna   just

          now blush pink   signifiers
of shade and hue limit my ability
to describe watercolour washed
over country still crowded with
Indigenous knowledge.

You never really understand
until you live it
          conceptualising distance is
          more corporeal than cerebral.

This is not home.   No blue mountain
crevices' strong valleys plateau edged
by my past   only colour
remains familiar against the
disconcerting lack of fence lines

below the QANTAS FIFO shuffle
a dead ocean scoured clean by
geological time sores cross-sectioned
with straight cut lines graded by
company men of and from
the past   yesterday's
exploration transect flails
an enduring scar.   Landscape

no longer heals. Either way nothing
changes linear paths turn left
or right become events of west and
east under the aeroplane wing
they disappear

                              nowhere
reappear   scrape an open-cut's
cyanic lake deep azure copper green
floods the next beside the tailings dam
faded orange bleeds a contrast.

You can't see corporate wealth
from a FIFO shuffle.   Foreign ownership
or family injunctions distil, form
residual patterns   folding palette pools
into false pigment waiting for the dip
and drip of a fine point brush.

Lost baseline. The
geology of the West.

Leaving Flores

volcanoes expose a horizon rising through haze
to straddle an imaginary line spliced through
this continent of islands. here Wallace grasped

his future. displaced God. found truth. here
where one biota nudges the next Eurasia
leans forward, ever so lightly she kisses

Austronesia: that ancient duality old
Sunda and Sahul⁴, her kiss so brief only
a whisper of Eurasian lip floats on the scent

of spices hanging lucid in the warm air
over Lombok Strait, aah *Nusantara* below
your currents thrill to a rush rich with nutrients

deeper than evolution. life. here too rest the old
Gods, watching *Ibu* stands to one side of *Bapak*
old *'Pak* smoking a *Kretek*, loudly clears earth's

throat. eons pass between his coughs: *'Pak* doesn't
wait for a concept of time to be created. no concept
ever thought lasts when your work is the making

of land. here wait Tambora, Rinjani, Agung, Batur
and that rebel alone, Sangeang Api, her brief appearance
as a sunset silhouette, with plans to grow like her cousin

Anak Krakatau: explosive — as if islands could flow
between ribbons of sunset and grey-blue haze, but it
is still *'Pak* Agung's smoke now lacing its way up

through this dense, cold air. crossing Wallace's line
we turn. descend. Denpasar airport
the height of the season

SIEV221 File Note: to mothers waiting[5]

If this was a different page
in the novel of Christmas Island
this would be the postcard beach.
A rough track curves down dark

cut cliffs rock ledges small
spit of sand calm shallows
sunshine Waterfall Bay
just around the headland

the Indian Ocean bites
makes sea caves hollow but
this year this end of the track
descends to tussock laced

between the ankle-risk
of burrows. Robber crabs
protect their scrapes.
Now an unexpected

abundance cast up wedged
between sea rocks and
guano flotsam rattling crisp
like old bones a cliché

too far perhaps its just
so many children's flip-flops
confuse why this midden
doesn't make sense why

colours shapes sizes cast up
in Waterfall Bay are the same
as those in the back streets
of Kuta and hanging dead

the Brown Booby reeks. It
turns on an ocean
updraft one wing
caught by discarded

fishing line trapped by the
same cliffs. A seabird's
gaze your child's last
witness.

Notes

.

¹ In November 2019, the 'Currowan' was ignited by lightning strike 20 kilometres north west of Batemans Bay, it burnt for 74 days, across 499,621 hectares destroying during what has been termed Australia's 'Black Summer' (Source: NSW RFS). In the village of Conjola Park and vicinity, around 130 homes were lost to this fire on New Year's Eve and three residents died as a direct result of the fire.

² Brindi's – the Brindabella Range, which borders NSW and the ACT.

³ Sunda and Sahul, ancient landmasses exposed during the last ice age, Sunda is partly in Indonesia and Sahul is made up of the present islands of Australia and New Guinea. Between them lies the 'Wallace Line' – a biogeographical boundary between the present day islands of Bali and Lombok.

⁴ On 15 December 2010 an Indonesian fishing boat, named SIEV 221 by Australian authorities, crashed onto rocks on Christmas Island and sank, 50 asylum seekers drowned, 14 were children (Source: *WA Inquest into the deaths of SIEV221 Christmas Island*, 23 February 2012).

Acknowledgements

Some of these poems (or earlier versions) were previously published in:

All Living Language, 2015.
ANU Poets' Luncheon 2000, Aberrant Genotype Press, 2000.
Artlook 2, 2004.
Australian Poetry Anthology 6, 2018 and 8, 2020.
Axon: Creative Explorations 9(2), 2019.
Breath of the Sea, Peter Cowan Writers Centre (PCWC), 2012.
Brushstroke II: Ros Spencer Poetry Contest Anthology 2020-21, WA Poets Inc., 2021.
Creatrix 28 and 30, WA Poets Inc., 2015.
FIRST, Faculty of Communication at UC, 1998.
foam:e 18, Oct/Nov, 2021.
fourW twenty-eight: New Writing 2017; thirty: PEARL 2019; thirty-three: NEW WRITING 2022.
Grieve: stories and poems about grief and loss 7, 2019.
Meniscus 6(2), 2018.
Poetry New Zealand 33, 2006.
Resilience: 2021 ACU Prize for Poetry, Australian Catholic University (ACU), Oct 2021.
StylusLit 7, Sept 2020.
34- 37 Degrees South 2022, Digital Anthology South Coast Writers Centre (SCWC), 2022.
Science Write Now 6, March 2022.
Uneven Floor 5, Feb 2018.

Westerly, 66.1, July 2021.

Westerly: New Creative Online Special Issue, Sept 2016;

Westerly: FROM THE EDITORS DESK #authorsforfireys, March 2020.

Writ Poetry Review 4, April 2020.

're/ main/ s' was written during a SCWC Emerging and Established Writers Bundanon Retreat 2022, and was awarded Highly Commended in the Lambing Flat FAW Poetry Competition 2022.

'Firepit' shortlisted for the ACU Prize for Poetry 2021.

'Part of its trunk' won the June Shenfield National Poetry Award 2020.

'Sydney to Perth: chasing dusk' was Commended for the Ethel Webb Blundell Literary Award 2020.

'This naked lake', 'Pyrocumulonimbus' and 'Fire Rites' were written during a 'Writing Fire Writing Drought' fellowship at Varuna, Katoomba, in October 2020.

'east west cast west cast west east' shortlisted for the Booranga Prize 2019.

'Aubie: Kokoda: 1988' won the Copyright Agency Ltd best poem in *Meniscus* 6(2) 2018.

'Flying W. A.' placed second for Ethel Webb Blundell Literary Award 2018.

'Too Many Years a Railway Daughter' was Highly Commended for the Patrons Prize (Peter Cowan Writers Centre) 2014.

'Washerwomans Beach' was longlisted for the South Coast Writers Centre Poetry Award 2022.

'Whitford Nodes Park: what I hear' was Highly Commended for the Glen Phillips Poetry Prize 2013.

Bio

Elanna Herbert was born and spent many years living and working in Canberra. She has also lived on the outskirts of a small rural village in the Yass valley of New South Wales and in Perth, Western Australia. She now lives and writes from Yuin country on the south coast of New South Wales. Elanna's work appears in numerous journals and anthologies. She won the June Shenfield National Poetry Award (2020) and shortlisted for the Australian Catholic University (ACU) Prize for Poetry (2021). She has twice been the runner up for Queensland Poetry's Emerging Older Poets' Mentorship Award.

Previous books include a collection of short fiction, *Frieda and the Cops* (Ginninderra Press, 2005) the manuscript of which won the Marion Eldridge Award (National Foundation for Australian Women) and an academic monograph *Neohistorical Fiction and Hannah's Place: A Creative Response to Colonial Representation* (VDM Verlag, 2008). Elanna holds a Doctorate in Communication from the University of Canberra.